Critical Thinking

Strategies for Decision Making

Daniel A. Feldman, Ph.D.

A Crisp Fifty-Minute™ Series Book

This Fifty-Minute™ book is designed to be "read with a pencil." It is an excellent workbook for self-study as well as classroom learning. All material is copyright-protected and cannot be duplicated without permission from the publisher. *Therefore, be sure to order a copy for every training participant through our Web site, www.axzopress.com.*

Critical Thinking

Strategies for Decision Making

Daniel A. Feldman, Ph.D.

CREDITS:
VP, Product Development: **Adam Wilcox**
Editor: **Ann Gosch**
Production Editor: **Genevieve McDermott**
Production Artists: **Nicole Phillips and Betty Hopkins**

Trademarks
Crisp Fifty-Minute Series is a trademark of Axzo Press.

Some of the product names and company names used in this book have been used for identification purposes only and may be trademarks or registered trademarks of their respective manufacturers and sellers.

Disclaimer
We reserve the right to revise this publication and make changes from time to time in its content without notice.

ISBN 10: 1-56052-648-3
ISBN 13: 978-1-56052-648-3
Library of Congress Catalog Card Number 2001098169
Printed in the United States of America

11 12 13 14 15 09 08

Learning Objectives For:

Critical Thinking:
Strategies for Decision Making

The objectives for *Critical Thinking: Strategies for Decision Making* are listed below. They have been developed to guide you the user to the core issues covered in this book.

THE OBJECTIVES OF THIS BOOK ARE TO HELP THE USER:

1) Explore the differences between critical and non-critical thinking

2) Learn strategies for improving the thinking necessary to make effective decisions at work

3) Understand how to evaluate the validity of arguments

4) Understand the role that evidence plays in supporting strong arguments and explanations

5) Formulate effective explanations with solid information and reasoned hypotheses

ASSESSING PROGRESS

A Crisp Series **assessment** is available for this book. The 25-item, multiple-choice and true/false questionnaire allows the reader to evaluate his or her comprehension of the subject matter.

To download the assessment and answer key, go to www.axzopress.com and search on the book title.

Assessments should not be used in any employee selection process.

About the Author

Dr. Daniel A. Feldman, president of Leadership Performance Solutions, is a consulting psychologist who has worked with corporate, government, and nonprofit organizations for more than 20 years.

Dr. Feldman helps organizations improve their effectiveness through leadership development, change management, and team building and has designed and facilitated a wide variety of human-capital development programs. In his role as an executive coach and facilitator, Dr. Feldman has the ability to bring a depth of understanding to the essential skills for workplace success.

Dr. Feldman is the author of *The Handbook of Emotionally Intelligent Leadership* and *The Manager's Pocket Guide to Workplace Coaching.* He is a frequent speaker on the topics of leadership, critical thinking, emotional intelligence, and coaching. Dr. Feldman received his doctorate in psychology from Virginia Commonwealth University.

For information about programs and presentations based on this book, contact:

Leadership Performance Solutions
Falls Church, Virginia
703-534-4300
dafeldman@mindspring.com

How to Use This Book

This *Fifty-Minute™ Series Book* is a unique, user-friendly product. As you read through the material, you will quickly experience the interactive nature of the book. There are numerous exercises, real-world case studies, and examples that invite your opinion, as well as checklists, tips, and concise summaries that reinforce your understanding of the concepts presented.

A Crisp *Fifty-Minute™ Series Book* can be used in a variety of ways. Individual self-study is one of the most common. However, many organizations use *Fifty-Minute* books for pre-study before a classroom training session. Other organizations use the books as a part of a systemwide learning program—supported by video and other media based on the content in the books. Still others work with Crisp to customize the material to meet their specific needs and reflect their culture. Regardless of how it is used, we hope you will join the more than 20 million satisfied learners worldwide who have completed a *Fifty-Minute Book*.

Preface

This book offers step-by-step guidance for strengthening the thinking skills necessary to grapple with the deluge of information we face daily, particularly at work. How can you determine the validity of an argument given by a co-worker? How can you explain the underlying cause of a shift in customer demand or the importance of a work process?

This book contains three parts. Part 1 introduces critical thinking and presents the pitfalls of non-critical thinking tactics. It explores the differences between ineffective and effective thinking styles and gives overall strategies for developing critical thinking.

Part 2 focuses on recognizing and evaluating arguments. It teaches the importance of recognizing the elements of an argument and the methods for judging the validity of an argument. It also gives direction for presenting effective arguments.

Part 3 enumerates steps for developing and evaluating explanations. It describes how to gather and process information and develop and test hypotheses. It also describes common errors in information processing.

Do you want to learn overall strategies for improving your critical thinking skills? If so, practice the exercises in Part 1.

Are people trying to convince you to adopt their point of view? If so, use the steps in Part 2 for recognizing and evaluating arguments.

Do you want to understand and explain a situation? If so, follow the steps in Part 3 for developing and evaluating explanations.

Together, the three parts of this book offer valuable guidance on how to make effective decisions in the workplace.

Daniel Feldman, Ph.D.

Acknowledgments

Much appreciation to Jeff Kelly for his insights and assistance. Enduring thanks to all my family—in particular my wife, Jo—for their tremendous support and encouragement. Heartfelt gratitude to Gurumayi Chidvilasananda for her continual loving guidance.

Contents

Part 3: Developing and Evaluating Explanations

Appendix

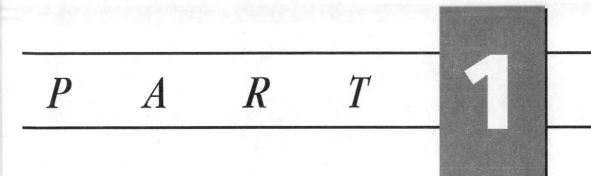

PART 1

Understanding Critical vs. Non-Critical Thinking

2

The Case for Critical Thinking

We live and work in a world of ever-accelerating change, where information is multiplying exponentially and job requirements are constantly shifting. More than ever, we must be able to reasonably challenge "standard operating procedure" or workflow processes. Faced with frequent choices about strategy and direction, employees today need the skills of critical thinking to choose the most effective path.

Decision-Making at Work

At work, we are faced regularly with information about which we must make decisions. For example, imagine Bob approaches you and says in a very serious tone,

> *"If you put that conclusion in the report, you'll be looking for a new job by Monday! The boss never likes new ideas. Look what happened to Chris. He's out on the street now."*

How should you respond to this statement? How much weight should you give it in deciding what to put in the report? Should you accept Bob's comments at face value and change what you wrote? Should you ignore it? What should you believe?

While trying to decide the correct path, we often develop explanations and evaluate statements that may or may not be true or that may be true but not relevant. Co-workers try to persuade us to adopt a particular point of view, and we present our ideas and opinions to persuade them. We also generate a host of ideas and statements within our own minds:

> *"We should form an action team for this initiative."*

> *"I think it would be best to focus on the needs assessment rather than the financial report."*

> *"I think the finance department isn't appreciated by the rest of the staff because no one sees their work."*

How can we successfully evaluate all this information to make effective decisions at work? With the power of critical thinking.

Benefits of Critical Thinking

Critical thinking involves evaluating a situation, problem, or argument and choosing a path of investigation that leads to finding the best possible answers. Listed below are a number of benefits that come from practicing critical thinking at work. Put a check (✔) by the three benefits that you would most like to bring to your job.

❏ Recognizing your own biases to guide self-improvement

❏ Contributing to teams through what you say and do

❏ Gaining the respect of both your manager and your co-workers

❏ Developing the best solutions to problems

❏ Gaining greater insight into the motives of others

❏ Giving sound arguments to create buy-in for your ideas

❏ Identifying key issues without getting sidetracked

❏ Writing and speaking with impact

❏ Improving customer service through greater understanding of customer needs

This book will provide you with a set of guidelines and skills for critical thinking. But first, let's look at the alternative and see what can happen when *non*-critical thinking is used.

THE PITFALLS OF NON-CRITICAL THINKING

Below is a list of pitfalls that can occur from non-critical thinking. Put a check (✔) by each one you or a colleague at work has fallen into in the past month. For each one identified, write what happened and the consequences.

For example, under "stupid mistakes" you might write:

What happened: *HR failed to tell staff about the changes in leave policy.*

Consequences: *All the timesheets had to be redone.*

❏ **Stupid mistakes**

What happened: _____

Consequences: _____

❏ **Promoting a dud of an idea**

What happened: _____

Consequences: _____

❏ **Wrong decisions**

What happened: _____

Consequences: _____

❏ **Disputes and disagreements because of misinformation**

What happened: _____

Consequences: _____

CONTINUED

❏ **Wasted time from being sidetracked**

What happened: _____

Consequences: _____

❏ **Believing there was buy-in when there was not**

What happened: _____

Consequences: _____

Probably most of the pitfalls were due to non-critical thinking. Next we'll explore non-critical thinking tactics used to influence others, to avoid unwittingly agreeing to something that isn't based on sound reasoning.

Recognizing Deceptive Reasoning

We practice critical thinking when we use reasoning strategies carefully and deliberately to reach a decision about what to believe or do. When people operate in non-critical styles, they easily slip into errors in reasoning. Deceptive reasoning tactics distort the reasoning process. The tactics might be unintentional or intentional.

Deceptive reasoning techniques include:

➤ Using irrelevant facts

➤ Avoiding uncomfortable facts

➤ Oversimplifying

➤ Arguing from ignorance

➤ Appealing to the multitude

➤ Presenting a false cause

➤ Begging the question

➤ Attacking the person

➤ Creating a "straw man"

➤ Sliding down a slippery slope

Using Irrelevant Facts

Definition: Citing facts that have no pertinence to the matter at hand.

Example: *"We're going to have a new company president in the next few months, so we might as well take it easy until he is selected."*

How to handle using irrelevant facts: Point out the irrelevance of the fact.

> *"Yes, we are getting a new president, but I think that is irrelevant to the level of effort we put into the job."*

Avoiding Uncomfortable Facts

Definition: Knowing certain facts but avoiding them because they do not support your argument.

Example: All the major economic indicators suggest a slowdown in the general economy. Despite this, Henry says, *"The lessening in demand for our product seems most likely related to the lack of effective marketing from the marketing department. Hence, the cutback of 20% of the staff there."*

How to handle avoiding uncomfortable facts:
Point out the missing fact.

> *"You know, Henry, there has been a major slowdown in the economy. I wonder if this is one factor you haven't considered."*

Oversimplifying

Definition: Making something sound less complex to the point of error.

Example: *"The increase in workload, the hiring freeze, and the reduction in benefits happened because the senior staff likes to shake things up."*

How to handle oversimplifying: Point out the illogic and mention other evidence that suggests a more complicated argument.

> *"I'm not sure that would be the only reason for the senior staff to make all those changes. I suspect major changes in company policy are influenced by many factors."*

Arguing from Ignorance

Definition: Taking a position based on the fact that it has never been disproved.

Example: *"I've never seen a more efficient way to go about it, so I guess this workflow process is the best there is."*

How to handle arguing from ignorance: Explain the limitations this has for proving a point.

> *"I understand you haven't seen a better way. But if we ever want to improve something, it takes research and looking at new ideas."*

Appealing to the Multitude

Definition: Seeking agreement to an idea because it is supported by a great number of people.

Example: *"We should use X brand printer paper because most people use it."*

How to handle appealing to the multitude: Mention the lack of support the statement has for the conclusion.

> *"That's like saying '50 million people can't be wrong!' Well, sometimes they can be! X brand paper may be popular, but that has nothing to do with the unique specifications and requirements of our printers."*

Presenting a False Cause

Definition: Claiming that one event causes another simply because it happens at around the same time.

Example: Valentina is friendly and outgoing. Jonathan is more introverted and quiet. Shortly after they are moved into a new workspace, Jonathan becomes less productive at work. Jonathan's supervisor says, *"Jonathan's work is suffering because Valentina talks too much."*

This is a false cause because no corroborating facts link the move to Jonathan's decreased efficiency. It could be due to his having a hard time changing in general or getting a new task that he does not know how to handle. Perhaps he has personal difficulties that happened to start about the same time as the move.

How to handle presenting a false cause: Point out the lack of connection that exists in the statement.

> *"Moving in with Valentina may have affected Jonathan's work, but so far there has been no proof there is any relationship between her talkativeness and his effectiveness."*

Begging the Question

Definition: Making a claim that is supported only by itself. This is also known as circular reasoning.

Example: *"You be the note taker and I'll be the leader for the meeting."*
"Why should you be the leader for the meeting?"
"Because you'll be taking the notes!"

How to handle begging the question: Challenge the reasoning and ask for a more convincing piece of evidence.

> *"Let's start from the beginning without either of us having an assigned role. Now, I'd like to discuss the criteria we want for a leader for this meeting."*

Attacking the Person

Definition: Falsely discounting an argument by discrediting the person making it.

Example: *"Janet says she has found a flaw in the financial analysis. I don't trust her judgment because Janet doesn't have a college degree."*

How to handle attacking the person: Point out the irrelevance these attacks have to the argument.

> *"Janet's not having a degree isn't relevant to this particular piece of work. Let's focus on the reasons she gives for the mistake."*

Creating a "Straw Man"

Definition: Distorting the conclusion of another and then attacking that misrepresented position.

Example:

> Josh: *"I think we should not keep working into the evening because we are more alert during the day."*

> Kathy : *"Josh is suggesting we don't have the character to handle the extra work load. Personally, I resent this attack on my dedication. I think we are an extremely committed group and should keep working into the night."*

How to handle creating a "straw man": Refocus on the original position.

> Josh: *"I also think we are a committed group. But my point had nothing to do with character or commitment and everything to do with effectiveness."*

Sliding Down a Slippery Slope

Definition: Arguing against a conclusion by implying it is linked to another conclusion even though the link between the two is tenuous or weak.

Example: *"If we give employees flex time, they will expect more and more benefits and eventually we'll be giving them a four-day workweek!"*

How to handle sliding down a slippery slope: Examine each conclusion one at a time.

> *"Giving employees flex time may or may not lead them to expect more benefits. If they do expect more benefits, this may or may not lead them to ask for a four-day workweek. Let's look at each of these points one at a time."*

Detecting Emotional Manipulation

We all come across emotional manipulations regularly. Techniques that fall into this category attempt to sway others primarily through emotions. Being aware of these techniques arms us against being dragged into the manipulation. At the same time, the use of emotionally manipulative tactics does not automatically invalidate the case being presented. Pick and choose what makes sense.

Emotional manipulation techniques include:

➤ Inflammatory words

➤ Pressure tactics

➤ Appeals to sentiment

➤ Ridicule

Inflammatory Words

Definition: Arousing or expressing feelings of approval or disapproval to get others to concede. Inflammatory words evoke emotions that may be untrue or irrelevant to the situation under review.

Example: *"He's a 'B' player."*
"That's a radioactive assignment."
"She's a clock watcher."

How to handle inflammatory words: Rephrase them into more neutral words, which forces the speaker to consider and clarify the message she is conveying. This helps you both to determine if the statement is relevant or accurate. For example:

Following *"He's a 'B' player,"* you could say, *"Do you mean he has been less productive than his co-workers?"*

To *"That's a radioactive assignment,"* you could respond, *"Do you mean it is a difficult and politically sensitive assignment?"*

After *"She's a clock watcher,"* you could ask, *"Do you mean she works the minimum amount of time required?"*

Pressure Tactics

Definition: Intimidating others into agreement.

Example: *"You'll make your boss unhappy."*
"The whole office will see you as a pariah."

How to handle pressure tactics: Ignore them. If this does not work, restate them in a neutral manner and ask for clarification. For example:

To *"You'll make your boss unhappy,"* you might respond, *"In what way will the boss be unhappy?"*

After *"The whole office will see you as a pariah,"* you could ask, *"Whom do you mean by 'the whole office' and what will they not like?"*

Appeals to Sentiment

Definition: Using pity or compassion to get others to accept particular conclusions.

Example: *"Bob should get a raise because he has eight kids."*

How to handle appeals to sentiment: Shift the conversation back to the argument at hand. For example, in responding to *"Bob should get a raise because he has eight kids,"* you might say, *"I realize Bob has a large family. But is he the best person for the job?"*

Ridicule

Definition: Saying something to make others appear contemptible as a way of forcing them to concede to a position.

Example: *"Why do you want to appear ignorant by not agreeing with rest of us?"*

How to handle ridicule: Point out the ridicule and question it. For example, in response to *"Why do you want to appear ignorant by not agreeing with everyone else?"* You might say, *"'Appearing ignorant' is a strong accusation. What do you mean by that?"*

TIP: *Emotional manipulation in and of itself may provide important information about a situation. It just doesn't provide evidence in support of the conclusion of the argument.*

CASE STUDY: The Manipulative Memo

Read the following memo. Circle and label any emotional manipulation tactics you detect.

Meg, the memo's author, is a technical consultant working on a project for a large government agency. She has written this memo to Allen, a technical consultant from a different consulting company, who is working on the same project.

> Dear Allen,
>
> I am writing this memo because I am concerned about the explosive e-mail you sent last week and hope you will send out a retraction of some of your key points.
>
> Based on what you wrote, I thought you overreached your authority and I am afraid that if I go to the senior project manager about this, he would agree with me. This would seriously impair the ability of your company to participate with other projects at this agency.
>
> The fact that you sent the e-mail to all of the project participants supports the impression that you have only a rudimentary understanding of the appropriate channels of communication.
>
> Meg

Rewrite the memo in a more neutral tone without using emotional manipulation tactics.

_____

_____

_____

_____

_____

_____

_____

_____

EXERCISE: EXAMINING THE EMOTION

Write a statement someone made to you this week that included an emotional manipulation tactic, such as "I'm sick and tired of upper management moving us around like pawns."

_____

_____

Ask yourself: What is the emotional impact of the specific words used in this statement?

_____

_____

_____

_____

Styles of Non-Critical Thinking

As you have learned, *non*-critical thinking is black and white, dogmatic and uninformed. It is passive, shallow, and reactive. Non-critical thinking operates from a narrow and limiting frame of reference, with continual pressure to doubt or exclude new ideas or ways of doing things.

A common feature of non-critical thinking is a refusal to evaluate objectively our own thought process, which shows up in several ways:

➤ "Closed-minded" thinking, which involves rigidly adhering to a previous point of view regardless of new evidence presented

➤ Excessive receptivity to every new idea presented in the mistaken belief that all opinions are equally valid

➤ Lazy thinking, which is a failure to analyze ideas fully

The various forms of non-critical thinking can be grouped in particular styles. Anyone can fall into any of the non-critical ways of thinking some of the time. We might fall into a particular style depending on the circumstances, such as being in a planning session with the manager or dealing with an unfamiliar situation. Some people, however, operate in one of these styles most of the time.

The Grinch	Closed-minded Suspicious Overly stubborn Rigid
The Dilettante	Overly receptive Vague Resents discipline Distractible
The Snob	Self-deluded Arrogant Excessively confident in his own conclusion Egotistical
The Emoter*	Vacillates between beliefs according to changing mood Reacts purely emotionally Does not look at underlying assumptions Makes excuses Does not examine the details of an argument
The Leech	Latches onto whatever someone else thinks Accepts information uncritically Avoids difficult problems Is lazy Is passive and dependent

*This is not to say that emotions are not useful. When employed appropriately, they are part of the critical thinking process. See p. 24.

NON-CRITICAL STYLES IN ACTION

In the spaces provided, identify the non-critical thinking styles demonstrated by the following stories and write how you determined that style.

1. Zack is a computer programmer. He has an opinion about everything and will comment on anything under discussion. His co-worker Juanita is a Web site developer. When asked if he thinks Juanita could handle a sophisticated assignment, Zack says,

   "How could she? She's only a Web site developer. Everybody knows they aren't real techies."

   Zack's non-critical thinking style(s)

   _____ Arrogant   Snob _____

   _____

2. Holly to Arjun:

   "I agree with your plan for the Ballard project. It sounds great."

   Later, after talking about it with another co-worker, Simon, she says to Arjun,

   "I have grave concerns about the Ballard project. Simon doesn't believe it will fly."

   Holly's non-critical thinking style(s)

   _____ Leech _____

   _____

CONTINUED

3. Talking to the director of human resources, the senior executive says,

   "I respect your many years of experience and the report from the experts. However, I still think we should ask the opinion of everyone in the office before we decide on how to structure the new pay schedule so everybody can be happy."

   The senior executive's non-critical thinking style(s)

   _____ Dilletante _____

   _____

Compare your answers to the author's suggested responses in the Appendix.

TIP: *It is OK to make imperfect decisions sometimes. Remind yourself that developing critical thinking skills is an ongoing process. The only real mistake is failing to learn from your imperfect decisions.*

Critical Thinking Styles

Critical thinkers generally are open and recognize many shades of gray. They understand and use the skills of critical thinking to consider different frames of reference and operate with a continual push to find new ideas and options. But there are different individual styles of critical thinking, just as there are for non-critical thinking.

We can use more than one critical thinking style at a time. In fact, the more styles we use together, the better our critical thinking. These styles lead to a deeper understanding of the situation.

The Explorer	Looks at all sides of a situation or problem Identifies the core element of a problem or situation Is curious Seeks new developments
The Student	Is diligent Researches alternative solutions to problems Does homework Corrects errors
The Warrior	Accepts challenges Perseveres Faces difficult problems
The Navigator	Guides others Looks ahead Plans a course of action
The Detective	Questions own thoughts and actions Tolerates ambiguity Pursues the elusive element of fact

CRITICAL THINKING STYLE FILE

Which critical thinking styles are demonstrated by the following stories? Remember that a person can be demonstrating more than one critical thinking style at a time.

1. The project management team is under pressure from top management to speed up its work. At the next team meeting, the team leader says,

   "We should skip our usual action planning and just come up with some estimates for these jobs."

   Alexa, a team member, interjects,

   "I don't agree. If we do that, we could end up with disastrous results and waste more time. I suggest that we look at how we can speed up our meeting format without sacrificing important steps in our decision-making."

   Alexa's critical thinking style(s)

   _____ Warrior

   _____

2. Pascal says,

   "I don't think we should automatically go along with the consultant's recommendations. We should ask more questions about how they came up with these results and what the consequences will be if we do or do not implement these changes. I'd be willing to meet with them and discuss all the details of how they came up with these suggestions."

   Pascal's critical thinking style(s)

   _____ explorer

   _____

CONTINUED

3. Chandrika says to her manager, Steven,

"I can't format the regulations until George gets me his part of the job. He's always late and it is very frustrating. I think he's just unmotivated and lazy."

Steven answers,

"Before we jump to conclusions, let's find out if there are other reasons why George is late. Perhaps there are factors we don't know about. I wonder what his perspective is? I'd like to talk to George and get more information about what might be going on."

Steven's critical thinking style(s)

_____

_____

4. On Hans' first day on the job, his new manager says,

"I know we hired you as a claims adjuster, but our budget analyst just quit and we need you to help out in this area as well. It will give you a new experience and be of great benefit to the company. We think you can handle it. What about it?"

After contemplating this idea for an hour, Hans goes to see his manager and says,

"Although I am excited about the claims adjuster work, I also would like to try taking on the additional responsibilities. I can't tell you for sure if I will be able to handle both jobs, even on a temporary basis, but I would like to see how it goes. Let's check in a week to see how it goes doing both, and maybe I'll have a clearer perspective about how it might work out long term."

Hans' critical thinking style(s)

_____

_____

Compare your answers to the author's suggested responses in the Appendix.

WHAT'S YOUR STYLE?

Taking another look at the non-critical and critical thinking styles, think about which styles you use most frequently.

Non-Critical Thinking Styles

The Grinch
The Dilettante ✓
The Snob — home
The Emoter
The Leech

Critical Thinking Styles

The Explorer ✓ ℍ
The Student
The Warrior ℍ
The Navigator ✓
The Detective

The non-critical thinking style I use most frequently is:

_____

_____

The critical thinking style I use most frequently is:

_____

_____

In the next section, you will learn four strategies to help you expand your critical thinking styles and go beyond your non-critical thinking tendencies.

Becoming a Critical Thinker

It is one thing to understand the benefits of critical thinking, but quite another to put critical thinking to work. When making decisions, apply these four strategies to help you increase your critical thinking:

Strategy 1: *A willingness to look at yourself*

Strategy 2: *Persistent evaluation*

Strategy 3: *Ongoing fair-mindedness*

Strategy 4: *Commitment to an informed decision*

Each of these strategies involves a series of steps, but you cannot devise an exact formula for every decision you must make. Just remember, when you are thinking critically, you should run through these steps. With effort and practice this approach to critical thinking will become automatic.

Strategy 1: A Willingness to Look at Yourself

As much as possible, practice honest self-awareness and reflection. You can improve your thinking and learning by looking at how you are thinking. You can challenge limiting, habitual styles of thinking and find new ways to look at each situation.

To begin the process of critical thinking you must first look at your thoughts. Focusing on your thinking can take effort and sometimes can be uncomfortable. When faced with a workplace challenge, you can decide to focus just on the easier parts of the task you are familiar with or you can focus on what you need to learn to succeed. You can respond to a problem in the same old way, or you can look at the patterns of how you think about the problem and discover a newer, improved strategy for dealing with it.

Steps for this strategy:

1. Ask *why* questions.

Instead of accepting things at face value, keep asking *why* you believe or view things as you do.

2. Identify and challenge your biases.

Biases and stereotypes encourage inaccuracies in perception. Holding onto them is a way to avoid using your "thinking muscles." Once you have identified your biases, exercise your "thinking muscles" as you go through the reasoning steps presented later in this book.

3. Recognize your thinking process, and get rid of unproductive thinking strategies and learn effective new ones.

People use different strategies for how they approach new information, problems, and challenges. Parts 2 and 3 of this book provide approaches that may give you new ideas for your thinking strategies.

Activities:

1. Keep a journal. It does not have to be a chronological diary. Use it as a place to have a conversation with yourself.

2. Schedule 30 minutes a week to review decisions over the past week in which you failed to use critical thinking. Practice the steps for evaluating arguments and explanations with each decision.

3. Look at yourself in the mirror (literally!). Ask yourself:

   What decisions have I made recently in a rushed or superficial way?

   _____

   What do I need to face today that I did not face yesterday? _____

   _____

   How have my biases affected my decisions? _____

   _____

4. Look for your stereotypes. Identify a generalization you hold about work that may be a limiting stereotype (for example, people on the administrative side of the business are not as important as those in the service side).

   _____

   _____

   Is this generalization absolutely true? _____

   _____

   How has this idea affected how I act at work? _____

   _____

   _____

   What would change if I held a different belief? _____

   _____

   _____

Strategy 2: Persistent Evaluation

Learn to actively examine and assess information. Use intellectual courage and perseverance to assess each step of dealing with an issue and to redirect your thinking as you go along.

Be clear about the criteria you are using to evaluate information. Check to see if it is comprehensive and relevant.

Steps for this strategy:

1. Solicit feedback from other sources.

You limit yourself when you evaluate events only from your own perspective. Regularly check documents or solicit perspectives from customers and co-workers.

2. Appraise the quality of possible answers.

Questions have answers that can be deemed either factually right or wrong (facts) or better or worse (opinions). Try to discover the best method for reaching correct or better answers.

3. Compare your initial goals with your results.

By touching base with your goals, you ensure your evaluation stays in line with what you want to accomplish.

Activities:

1. Ask trusted peers for their honest assessment about the progress of your most important current project.

2. Select an ongoing project at work to analyze.

   Ask yourself:

   How can I discriminate between what I really need to focus on to get the job done and what is not really relevant or essential?

   _____

   _____

   _____

3. The next time you are dealing with an issue at work, ask yourself: What is the closest example of this type of problem I have dealt with before? How did I deal with it that time?

   _____

   _____

   _____

4. Identify an area of vulnerability. Are you sensitive to criticism? Do you feel that you lean on your manager too much?

   Now ask yourself:

   How does this hinder my critical thinking?

   How can I get rid of this vulnerability?

   _____

   _____

   _____

Strategy 3: Ongoing Fair-Mindedness

Approach differing opinions with a respectful, open mind. Appreciate not only that many others have a different and useful perspective, but also that your own perspective may be limited or incorrect.

Steps for this strategy:

1. Accept that others may have a different worldview.

Imagine another person's world and upbringing–the values he was taught and the challenges he has faced. Put yourself in his shoes and then view the current situation from his perspective.

2. Look for points of agreement.

When you are having an argument or disagreement, focus on aspects of the opposing points that you could agree with.

3. Recognize there are often several solutions to a problem.

Never stop at your first solution. Approach every problem as if it is an assignment from a client who wants at least three solutions to choose from.

Activities:

1. Think of the colleagues or subordinates for whom you have the least respect. Schedule a time to meet with them and find what you can do to help them be more effective at their job. Learn what you can about their background and values, and try to walk in their shoes.

2. Identify a workplace controversy. Determine the different sides in the controversy. Write an argument for each side. Identify points of agreement.

3. Think of a solution you came up with in the past week. Develop three alternative solutions to the problem that use procedures not usually in your repertoire.

Strategy 4: Commitment to an Informed Decision

Research every important decision you will make as if you will be cross-examined by an expert in that field before a jury of your peers. Try to integrate all available information into your decision.

After everything is said and done, be willing to take a stand.

Steps for this strategy:

1. Create a clear line of reasoning.

Start from your basic assumptions, and build a logical step-by-step progression to the reasonable solution. Challenge each step in the final progression.

2. Go for the most probable answer rather than waiting for total accuracy.

There are too many unknowns in the world to be 100% sure of most things. When you have tested a hypothesis enough to have the courage of your convictions, go with it—while recognizing that it could be improved upon.

3. Recognize the need for trade-off or consensus in making your decision.

In other words, take the decision's social context into account. Remember that your decision must be implemented in the real world, not an idealized "virtual" world.

Activities:

1. Clearly spell out your reasons for some action you took at work this week.

   Action Taken:

   _____

   Reasons:

   _____

   _____

   Identify ways you could have gathered more information before taking this action.

   _____

   _____

2. List three decisions you currently need to make at work for which there is no absolute right or wrong answer.

_____

_____

_____

Analyze the most important one according to the three steps for committing to an informed decision.

Decision:_____

Trace your clear line of reasoning toward that decision.

_____

_____

Explain any misgivings you might have had before deciding to go with the most probably answer rather than waiting for total accuracy.

_____

_____

What trade-offs or consensus did you recognize in making your decision?

_____

_____

3. Identify the problem at work you would most like to resolve. Identify the barriers to resolving the problem. Write an action plan for overcoming those barriers.

Problem:_____

Action Plan: Overcoming the Constraints

_____

_____

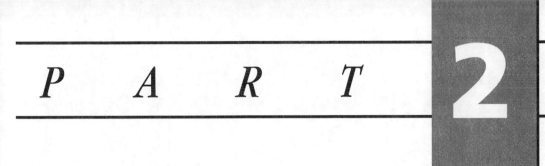

Recognizing and Evaluating Arguments

Defining Arguments

Throughout our day at work, we most often base our decisions on arguments or explanations about a situation. In this book, critical thinking is explored through the framework of these two aspects of thinking—arguments and explanations.

First, we will look at the framework for recognizing and evaluating *arguments*. We are not using the word *argument* to mean having a nasty face-off with someone. Instead, we are looking at the framework critical thinkers use to *persuade* someone of a position. Explanations are covered in Part 3.

Issues and Answers

In the workplace, we grapple every day with numerous issues requiring us to evaluate statements, complex situations, and conflicts. Critical thinking gives us a process for evaluating and understanding these issues.

When faced with a statement, we can choose to agree or disagree with it. In determining our acceptance or rejection of a statement, we enter into critical thinking. We evaluate a statement and look at the evidence that supports it.

Certain statements are easier to evaluate than others, such as *"It's raining outside"* or *"The network is down."*

The truth or falsity of other statements is more difficult to determine. These statements are more a matter of opinion. These are about *issues* on which reasonable people might disagree.

Example:

"People in sales are loners."

"We should change the strategic direction of the company."

The statements above each take a particular stand on an issue. These are called *conclusions*. A conclusion that is not agreed upon and is given supporting *evidence* for why it should be believed is called an *argument*.

Picturing an Argument

In critical thinking terminology, an argument is an attempt to support a disputed conclusion through evidence.

Think about the connections between these terms by imagining an argument as a table. The tabletop is the position taken, the conclusion. The pieces of evidence are the legs supporting the tabletop. Someone else might not agree that it is the correct tabletop. The purpose of the argument is to give supportive evidence for using that particular tabletop.

The Structure of an Argument

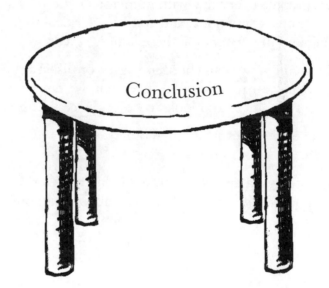

Example:

Your co-worker makes the statement, "Boy, this company is really going down the tubes. Our stock has tanked. Our customers are leaving us. Our profits are down and morale is the lowest I've ever seen it."

This is an argument because it presents a conclusion with supporting evidence. The issue is the state of the company.

Step-by-Step Analysis

To become critical thinkers, we must learn to recognize issues to better understand what is at stake. Then we can delve into understanding and analyzing arguments.

Recognizing and evaluating arguments involves seven steps as follows:

> **Step 1:** *Pinpointing Issues*
>
> **Step 2:** *Identifying Arguments*
>
> **Step 3:** *Seeking Clarity*
>
> **Step 4:** *Understanding Context*
>
> **Step 5:** *Finding Credibility*
>
> **Step 6:** *Looking for Consistency*
>
> **Step 7:** *Judging Arguments*

Let's look at each step in depth.

Step 1: Pinpointing Issues

People at work are continually trying to shape our beliefs and behaviors. If we are unaware of the underlying issues being presented, we may end up acting in ways we would not have if we had thought about the issues more deeply. Consequently, the first step in critical thinking is to figure out what the actual issue is.

Communication can often be confused and muddled, so identifying the issue can also help clarify a situation. Jack Kilby, the inventor of the microchip, has said, "A lot of solutions fail because they're trying to solve the wrong problem."

The first step to applying critical thinking to a topic is to ask: What is the real issue?

What Is the Issue?

The issue is the topic under discussion. It is any matter of controversy or uncertainty. It is the focus, the main point, the problem, or the question in dispute.

Identifying the issue means focusing on the central concept of the information being presented.

When trying to identify the issue, be neutral and objective. An issue is best-stated in question format and in a way that can be answered either for or against the issue.

Let's go back to the statement that began this book.

Bob approaches you and says in a very serious tone,

> *"If you put that conclusion in the report, you'll be looking for a new job by Monday! The boss never likes new ideas. Look what happened to Chris. He's out on the street now."*

What is the issue under discussion? (Remember to state the issue as a question, and format it in a way that can be answered either for or against the issue.)

_____

_____

Suggested answer:

Objectively stated, the issue is: Should that particular conclusion be kept in the report?

Note that the issue is stated in a nonjudgmental way that can be answered affirmatively or negatively.

Steps to Pinpointing the Issue

➤   Be neutral and objective.

➤   State the issue in a question format that can be answered yes or no.

➤   Review your formulation of the issue with the information that has been presented to you.

Identify the issue in the following examples:

1. You receive the following e-mail from your organization's information technology department:

   ```
   Because of security concerns and low usage, we have con-
   cluded that it would be best to discontinue remote access
   (dial-up access) to the Local Access Networks (LANs).
   ```

   Issue:

   _____

   _____

2. The safety officer at a metal finishing company makes the statement:

   "If we don't get everybody trained on how to handle those new cyanide platting baths, were going to get in trouble with the OSHA inspectors."

   Issue:

   _____

   _____

3. The creative services manager at an advertising agency leaves a note for the director saying:

   ```
   We are losing too much business because we have so many
   dinosaurs in this place. We need to bring in some new
   people with fresh ideas so we can stay competitive.
   ```

   Issue:

   _____

   _____

Suggested answers:

The issue is: Should we remove the remote access to the LANs?

The issue is: Do our employees need safety training?

The issue is: Do we need to restaff?

Pinpointing Discussion Issues

Sometimes in a conversation, people are discussing two separate issues without even realizing it. One person is talking about apples and the other about oranges. This can lead to hurt feelings, confusion, and major mistakes. Sometimes one party might purposely confuse the issue to win support. Or the party might attempt to avoid an aspect of the issue that she wants to obscure.

Example:

Dennis, a product manager for a telecommunications company, has been pushing the technical development department for the promised upgrades to a product he supports. He sends an e-mail requesting a clear timetable for the delivery of the upgrade. A return e-mail from the manager of the technical development department says,

```
The technical development department has a clear commit-
ment to create the best products possible. The response
from our customers has been outstanding. The high quality
of our products has been confirmed by our customers. We
want to work hand in hand with you to help you fully sup-
port the products. We want to thank you for all the good
work you have performed in communicating the effectiveness
of the company products.
```

The technical development department manager seems to be focusing on the quality of the department's work rather than the specific request for a timetable for the delivery of the upgrade.

Study the following case study and identify the issues present.

CASE STUDY: What Is the Issue?

The following discussion is between two employees at an office supply company. Jeff is a salesman and Doris is his manager.

Jeff: *"Doris, I'm fed up with George in the production department. He's failed to stick to his production commitments and I'm left holding the bag. I don't want to deal with him anymore."*

Doris: *"Have you discussed the problem with him?"*

Jeff: *"Why should I coddle him? He knows he's blown it."*

Doris: *"Maybe you can find out where the holdup is over there and help solve the problem."*

Jeff: *"I've got my job to do. I can't do his as well."*

Doris: *"I think it would be good if you met with George to discuss these difficulties."*

Jeff: *"Why are you siding with him rather than me?"*

Pinpoint the issues under discussion:

_____

_____

_____

_____

Compare your answers to the author's suggested responses in the Appendix.

Keeping the Issue in Focus

Staying focused on an issue during a discussion requires following three steps:

> ➤ Orally state the issue.

> ➤ Reach agreement on what the issue actually is.

> ➤ Refocus on the issue as needed.

In the case study on the previous page, what might Doris have said to stay on topic during the discussion?

Doris could have said, *"I think we are talking about two different issues. You are focused on convincing me that you shouldn't have to work with George. I'm focused on trying to solve the problem of the two of you not being able to work together. How about we take the broader perspective and look at how to solve the problem before we zero in on specific actions?"*

If there is disagreement, keep discussing until you have agreement about what issue you are going to talk about.

As you continue the discussion, keep focused on the issue. If the conversation moves away from the issue or gets muddled, bring everyone involved back to the agreed-upon issue or get agreement that you are focusing on a new issue.

TIP: *Regularly observe your own thinking to see if you are staying focused on the issue when you are arguing with yourself.*

Step 2: Identifying Arguments

How do you make sense of what you hear and read? How can you understand the reasoning behind what is being presented and look for the best, most reasonable answer? Most issues are presented with supporting evidence. After pinpointing the issue, you can then begin to analyze the underlying argument being presented.

In critical thinking, as in law, an argument is an attempt to support or prove a conclusion about an issue through evidence. Evidence consists of statements that provide support for the conclusion. Evidence communicates the *reasons* the presenter is for or against the issue.

When confronted with others' conclusions, you must decide if you want to make them your own conclusion. You cannot reach your own conclusion until you clarify the information being presented to you.

To reach your own conclusion on an issue, you must be able to identify the conclusions and evidence being presented.

Methods for Identifying Conclusions

➤ Look in likely locations—the beginning or end of a conversation or written documents.

➤ Look for word cues that introduce a conclusion, such as "thus," "consequently," "this shows that," "my point is," or "in short."

➤ If there is no clear statement within the body of what has been said or written, create a statement that answers the question "What is this about?" or "What is this person trying to prove?" or "What am I trying to prove?"

CASE STUDY: New Faces

Here is a letter from an employee, printed in a company newsletter:

It seems things have changed in the 20 years I've worked for this company. Unlike what I felt during most of my years here, today I feel a sense of discomfort when I come into work. There are a lot of new young faces around. I don't recognize most of them. They don't seem to make the effort to introduce themselves. All I hear is people thinking about how they can advance their own careers, not help the company. I'm not sure, but in my opinion this has hurt the efficiency of the company. I'd be interested in hearing what other people think about this.

What is the issue and the conclusion in this letter?

Issue:

_____

_____

Conclusion:

_____

_____

Compare your answers to the author's suggested responses in the Appendix.

Methods for Identifying Evidence

As we mentioned before, an argument is composed of a conclusion and evidence. We have learned how to locate the issue and the conclusion. The next step in understanding an argument is to locate the evidence being presented.

➤ Look for indicator cues that introduce statements of evidence:

Since…
For example…
Is supported by…
As shown by…
As a result of…
In view of…
As indicated by…
This is implied by…

➤ Ask the why question: "Why does that person say they take that position?"

TIP: *Be open to new reasons even if they do not fit your initial opinion.*

In the following case study, identify the *issue* and the *conclusion*, and then list the evidence given to support the *conclusion*.

CASE STUDY: Moving Toward the Internet

Acme, Inc., is a company that sells tools directly to garages and auto-supply stores. It recently started selling over the Internet. A senior manager writes the following memo to the vice president for operations.

> The future of this company is in Internet sales. More and more people are signing on and getting more at ease with performing tasks over the Internet.
>
> We have been selling our products over the Internet for the past 1 1/2 years. Over that time, Internet sales have increased 155% every six months. At the same time there has been a corresponding decrease in traditional sales of 15%. Our traditional sales methods carry an enormous overhead. Therefore, I believe we need to shift our strategic direction and weigh in much more heavily in support of the technical operations and marketing of Internet sales.

Identify the issues, conclusions, and evidence that support the conclusions.

Issue:

_____

_____

Conclusion:

_____

_____

Evidence:

_____

_____

Compare your answers to the author's suggested responses in the Appendix.

Step 3: Seeking Clarity

An important part of critical thinking involves assessing the value of evidence. Just looking at conclusions will not lead you to the truth. You must assess the strength of the reasoning behind the conclusion to determine if you should agree. This begins with discovering if you clearly understand what has been said or written.

You cannot get to the core of the points being made in an argument if the meaning of words and phrases is confusing. This confusion must be addressed before you can understand the substance of an argument.

Addressing Ambiguities

When you look closely at the words or phrases of an argument, you might discover several types of ambiguities.

The meaning of the words in the statement can be unclear and vague.

"Lots of employees take office supplies home with them."

In this statement, exactly how many employees does the word *lots* mean? Do a majority of employees steal office supplies and take them home or is it only three or four?

Words with unclear meaning should be clarified or avoided.

Words in a statement can have multiple meanings.

"There was a reaction in the lab that upset senior management."

This statement could refer to a chemical reaction in the laboratory or a reaction by the employees of the lab.

"All the good workers in the company work late."

What group of people are the "good workers"? Are they the best performers in the company or the workers who have the most positive values?

The word *late* is also vague because it is open to a wide range of interpretation. It could mean working until 5:30 P.M. instead of the standard 5 P.M. closing, or it could mean working until 10 P.M.

The meaning of words can be unclear within a particular context.

"We don't have the resources necessary to support that project."

Resources could refer to tangibles such as people and equipment, or it could refer to financial support.

Sentence structure can lead to ambiguity.

"Wanted: man to sell cars on discount."

Does the man work for a discount or are the cars at a discount?

Key Points:

➤ When you are able, follow up with the speaker or writer and ask her to clarify what she meant by a particular word or phrase. You can also ask for examples to better understand what she intended to say.

➤ Ambiguity that is not clarified weakens the argument. The greater the degree of ambiguity in an evidence statement, the less support it offers the conclusion.

REPHRASING FOR CLARITY

Identify the ambiguous words or phrases in the following statements, and explain how they are unclear. Rewrite the statements to make them clearer.

1. The (effect) of the (cutbacks) (reverberated) throughout the organization.

   Rewrite: *layoffs depressed the empolyees throughout of the*

   declined productn (10%)

   The effect of layoff increase   10%

   sick call by 10% throuh

2. In an e-mail:

   ```
   I do not appreciate your weak acknowledgment. Please
   take it back.
   ```

   Rewrite:

   _____

   _____

3. (Excessive) (time) on the phone (explains) the (lack) of (productivity.)

   Rewrite:

   More than 10 mn of the phone is the reason

   why 1st went down 10%

   Call backing decreased by

*Compare your answers to the author's suggested
responses in the Appendix.*

Step 4: Understanding Context

Many issues are easier to identify, clarify, and evaluate when we know the context in which they occur.

For example, the normal way of working in your office reflects the personal philosophy of the chief executive officer. In another office, however, the norm might be completely different. Thus, *normal* is a valid descriptor only in the *context* of your particular office.

The context involves:

➤ The presenter's motive and purpose

➤ The place

➤ The circumstances around the issue

The Presenter's Motive and Purpose

Part of the context involves the motive behind a spoken or written statement. It helps to ask: What is the real purpose behind what was said?

➤ Is the person pushing a personal point of view?

➤ Does my buy-in to this person's reasoning advance a personal agenda?

➤ Does my agreement make him look good? Will it better his lot?

➤ Is she under stress? Does she want the issue to "go away"?

CASE STUDY: What's Behind the Statement?

You are a new executive assistant at a law firm. Cal Bartlett is another executive assistant who has taken it upon himself to teach you the ropes. He says, *"The most important thing you can do to get kudos from the boss is to regularly run the status reports on the computer."*

What are Cal Bartlett's possible motives and purposes?

_____

_____

_____

_____

Compare your answers to the author's suggested responses in the Appendix.

The Place

The location of a communication can give you more information about the evidence. Ask yourself a variety of questions to see if the place has any relevance to the statement. These questions might include:

➤ Were co-workers around who were meant to hear this?

➤ Was it a location where the person would feel defensive, weak, or insecure?

➤ Was it in a setting in which the speaker would feel comfortable or uncomfortable?

➤ Was this e-mail copied to anyone else?

➤ If it was oral, who was in earshot?

➤ If it was written, who else would be reading it? Could it have been directed toward that other person?

Example:

Let's say someone sends you the following e-mail:

> I hope the assistance I gave you on the Brookings account was helpful. Let me know if there is anything else I can do. I'm always here to help.

What are some relevant questions to ask about this e-mail?

_____

_____

_____

TIP: *To assess the impact of place on an issue, picture the communication happening with a different audience to see if it would have played out the same way.*

Suggested answers:

Was the e-mail copied to someone else, such as the manager?

Was there a reason the person e-mailed you rather than just telling you face-to-face?

The Circumstances

The surrounding circumstances can influence the meaning of a piece of evidence.

Ask yourself: Are there other relevant factors that would strengthen my support for the issue?

Example:

> Robert sees you in the hall and says, *"This department has serious difficulties. The manager is inept. He has sullied our reputation among the other divisions. Everyone complains about the lack of communication. Customers are seriously thinking of going somewhere else."*

Upon investigation you discover that Robert had been asked to resign by his current manager. He had accepted a job with another company, and you did not know it at the time of the interaction.

Step 5: Finding Credibility

Credibility is the believability of a statement or position. Credibility helps you determine if evidence is true or false, adequate or inadequate. To help you determine credibility, you can turn to your own experience or that of others.

Uncovering Credible Evidence

When analyzing the credibility of an argument, ask three questions:

➤ Does the evidence conflict with my personal observations?

➤ Does the evidence conflict with my background knowledge?

➤ Is the source of the evidence credible?

Does the evidence conflict with my personal observations?

If some evidence conflicts with your own firsthand observation, its credibility should be in serious doubt. At the same time, you should be aware of the limits of your own observations. Sometimes your perception can be biased by a particular point of view. For example, if you really want something, it can influence you to perceive things in a way supportive of that event. Other times, circumstances can hinder effective observation, such as when you are trying to do two things at the same time.

Does the evidence conflict with my background knowledge?

Evidence can be compared to your own knowledge about the issue. The greater your knowledge on the subject, the weaker a conflicting piece of evidence should be seen. And obviously, the greater the conflict between the two, the less credible the evidence. At the same time, remember to keep an open mind to new information that may not fit with your own beliefs or understanding.

An example of an important place to assess credibility is the Internet. The Internet provides unfiltered information and thus can be the source of rumor, gossip, error, and deception, as well as useful information. It gives anyone the opportunity to publish anonymously in cyberspace material that could never before be accepted by the gatekeepers for reputable, established publishers.

Is the source of the evidence credible?

Often we might not be able to gather any additional information about an issue, so the credibility of the source is important because it is all we have to go on.

The more knowledgeable the source is about a given subject, the more reason there is to accept what the source has to say about it.

To help you determine the credibility of a source, ask the following questions:

➤ Did the source directly observe the situation or is the information simply hearsay?

➤ Are the events highly improbable?

➤ Is there supporting testimony?

➤ Is the source knowledgeable about the subject?

SHOULD THE COMPANY EXPAND?

You work at a pharmaceutical sales company and have received a report about expanding into a new region. The question is whether the company should open a new field office. The report gives a number of statements about why it would be good to jump into this region with a major capital investment. But some confusing evidence for the move calls into question the author's expertise.

How do you go about assessing the author's credibility?

_____

_____

_____

_____

_____

Let's assume that upon investigation you discover the following facts:

The author of the report would prefer to live in a town located in the new region. You discover that setting up field offices is not his area of expertise. He has had no experience setting up field offices and does not really know what is involved and the resources it would entail. He is the protégé of a senior executive who has been pushing for the move into this region for years.

How would you rate the overall credibility of this source?

_____

_____

_____

TIP: *Just because you have negative feelings about a person or you do not like a particular characteristic does not mean you should automatically discredit what that person has to say.*

Step 6: Looking for Consistency

Another way to help evaluate the argument is to look for consistency. Check to see if any pieces of evidence contradict other evidence or the conclusion or if the evidence is even relevant.

Contradictory Evidence

We can compare different pieces of evidence to see if they are contradictory.

Example:

You work as a loan processor in a mortgage finance company. You receive a report sent to the staff in your department from the closing department that has been disseminated to all of the staff in the loan department. It reads:

> The lack of timeliness on the part of your department impacts our department's productivity. We spend a lot of our time just waiting for the loan processors to finish their work. As everyone knows, we cannot do our job until the processors have done theirs. There are many different demands on our staff beyond that given to us by the processors. We are completely helpless and at the whim of when the processors decide to complete their tasks. Given this situation, we plan to request that the senior management establish tighter time standards for the turnover of relevant documents.

Analyze the structure of the report above and point out any inconsistencies in the evidence. Outline the argument on a separate piece of paper, using the headings below.

Issue:

Conclusion:

Evidence:

Inconsistencies:

Suggested answers:

Issue:

Should the time standards for document turnover be tightened?

Conclusion:

Yes, there should be tighter time standards for the loan processing department.

Evidence:

1. The loan processors' lack of timeliness impacts the closing department's productivity.

    a. The closing staff cannot do its work until the documents come from the processors.

    b. The closing staff spends a lot of its time waiting for finished documents from the loan processors.

2. The closing staff has many different demands on it beyond the work from the processors.

3. The closing staff is completely helpless and at the whim of the processors.

Inconsistencies:

Evidence #2 is inconsistent with evidence #1a. If there are other demands beyond the work from the processors, the closing staff could be working on those demands, or at least on work other than that requiring the documents from the loan department. Evidence #2 also conflicts with #3 because if the staff could be engaged in other work, it would not be completely helpless and at the whim of the processors.

This inconsistency suggests that tightening the time standards for document turnover may not really be what is needed to fix this problem.

True but Irrelevant Evidence

Sometimes the evidence can be true but irrelevant to the conclusion.

Example:

Gabriella is a property manager at a large apartment development. Burt, the engineering manager, reports to her. Gabriella has repeatedly spoken to him about being too aggressive with his employees. One of his employees tells her that Burt was yelling at him. When she confronts Burt about the incident, Burt tells her, *"I think I was justified in yelling at him because he was late for the third day in a row!"*

Is the evidence in this example consistent? Write supporting reasons for your answer.

_____

_____

_____

_____

_____

Suggested answer:

The evidence the engineering manager cited is probably true. The employee probably was late three mornings in a row. But the truth of the evidence in this case is irrelevant to the inappropriate aggression demonstrated by the engineering manager and thus is inconsistent with the argument.

Step 7: Judging Arguments

You now have the tools to avoid accepting arguments at face value. You can recognize the non-critical thinking tactics of deceptive reasoning and emotional manipulation and how to handle them. When you do, be assertive without becoming confrontational or hostile.

Assertive questioning means you do not passively accept or aggressively attack. When you passively accept the ideas and reasons of another or assert a position that has randomly popped into your head, you are thinking non-critically. When you attack, you are practicing emotional manipulation.

The previous six steps provide a framework for recognizing and evaluating an argument. Once you have pinpointed the issue and identified conclusions and evidence, you can answer these five questions for judging an argument:

1. Is the evidence clear and unambiguous?

2. Does the context strengthen or weaken the evidence?

3. Is the evidence credible?

4. Are all the pieces of evidence consistent with one another?

5. Does the evidence support the conclusions?

In the following case study, see if you can identify the issue, the conclusion being presented, and the evidence supporting the conclusion. Then examine and evaluate the strength of the evidence and the overall strength of the argument.

CASE STUDY: Should You Accept the Proposal?

You are a member of the submissions division of a grant-giving foundation. The submissions division is responsible for collecting grant proposals.

You have been given the following proposal for an internal process improvement. It was produced by an internal task force that included two information technology specialists, a records manager, an operations manager, and an HR specialist. The principal advocate for this initiative is the head of the information technology department, who recently transferred from the accounting department.

```
The operations of the division need to be streamlined and
strengthened to improve the way submissions from the public
are handled. This is important for both internal efficiency
and the satisfaction of our customers. There is a great need
to move toward solely electronic submissions.

Data storage is becoming cumbersome and expensive. The cur-
rent method of cataloging, handling, and so on is ineffi-
cient and prone to error. No data would be lost by dealing
only with electronic submissions. The Internet technology
that would facilitate electronic submission of the informa-
tion is now readily available to our entire customer base.
The electronic submissions would be properly organized so
they could be placed directly into our database without
requiring staff for data entry. Our customers would get
immediate acknowledgement of the receipt of their submis-
sions.

The system would quickly identify delinquent or errant sub-
missions. Our current databases are using yesterday's tech-
nology, and this will give us the opportunity to upgrade
them to today's accepted level.

The transition to such a program would take a maximum of 12
months and would begin to save the organization money within
three months of full operation.

It would reduce the current burden on staff so that staff
could begin to focus on other responsibilities.
```

62

Based on the case study on the previous page, write down your thoughts on the following:

Issue:_____

_____

Conclusion:_____

_____

Evidence:_____

_____

Analysis:

1. Is the evidence clear and unambiguous?

_____

2. Does the context strengthen or weaken the evidence?

_____

3. Is the evidence credible?

_____

4. Are all the pieces of evidence consistent with one another?

_____

5. Does the evidence support the conclusions?

_____

Compare your answers to the author's suggested
responses in the Appendix.

ARGUMENT ANALYSIS AT WORK

Select a complex argument from work like the preceding case study. Practice your critical thinking by going through this argument analysis form.

Issue:_____

_____

Conclusion:_____

_____

Evidence:_____

_____

Analysis:

1. Is the evidence clear and unambiguous?

_____

2. Does the context strengthen or weaken the evidence?

_____

3. Is the evidence credible?

_____

4. Are all the pieces of evidence consistent with one another?

_____

5. Does the evidence support the conclusions?

_____

Presenting Ideas Powerfully

By learning how to recognize and evaluate arguments, you also have learned tools to help you *present* effective arguments. If you have a good grasp of the issue and you present clear, credible, and consistent evidence that validly supports your conclusion, you will have the basis for a strong argument.

You must *present* your conclusions so they will stand up to critical analysis and be openly received.

Keys to Powerful Presentations

To present your ideas powerfully, by either speaking or writing, remember these key points:

> **Be prepared.**
>
> Being prepared means making the effort and time commitment for creating a good argument.

> **Have a clear idea of your position.**
>
> If you are not sure of your position, why should anyone else be swayed to it?

> **Have a clear intention of precisely what you want to accomplish.**
>
> Develop a clear goal for your presentation. What outcomes would you like to achieve?

> **Avoid ambiguities.**
>
> When people hear confusing or vague evidence, you lose your connection with them.

> **Stick to your issue.**
>
> The more complex the argument, the more difficult it is to stay focused on your issue. Remember to keep returning to your main point.

➤ **Know your audience.**

The more you understand your audience, the more you can pitch your ideas in their language and direct your pitch toward their areas of concern.

➤ **Present a balanced point of view.**

If you stridently push one perspective without discussing (and then challenging) opposing sides to the issue, you can polarize your audience against you.

➤ **Predict challenges and have prepared responses.**

Think ahead about how a listener or reader might try to shoot down your idea. Prepare and practice responses for dealing with these challenges.

➤ **Seek feedback from others.**

Bounce your ideas off a trusted colleague, if possible, to test your argument and refine your presentation.

Develop the body of your presentation by following these steps:

1. Spell out your argument.

2. Define key terms.

3. State your underlying assumption.

4. Group together your evidence for a given conclusion.

5. Proceed in an orderly direction: conclusion, main evidence, next evidence, conclusion.

6. Give examples.

7. Summarize at the end of a complete section and at the end of the entire presentation.

PRESENTATION CHECKLIST

Before your next written or oral presentation, run through the following checklist:

❏ How much time do I need to be effectively prepared?

_____ minutes/hours/days

❏ My clearly spelled-out bottom-line position is:

_____

_____

_____

❏ What is the ideal outcome from this presentation?

_____

_____

_____

❏ What are the most important facts about my audience?

_____

_____

_____

❏ What are the opposing viewpoints to my argument and how can they be challenged?

Viewpoint: _____

_____

Challenge: _____

_____

Viewpoint: _____

_____

Challenge: _____

_____

Viewpoint: _____

_____

Challenge: _____

_____

❏ Whom can I ask for feedback about my ideas before my written or oral presentation?

_____

68

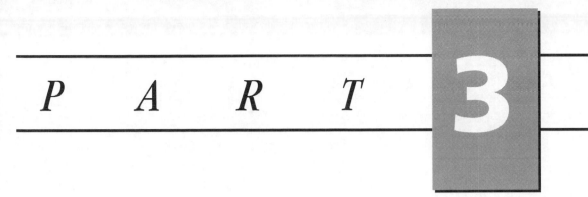

Developing and Evaluating Explanations

70

Explanations vs. Arguments

When we think critically, we take different approaches depending on whether we are trying to recognize and evaluate an *argument* or whether we are trying to develop or evaluate an *explanation*. But distinguishing between an argument and an explanation can be difficult.

While arguments attempt to persuade, explanations take the point of view of discovery and understanding. Thus, when people are trying to convince you to adopt their point of view, you use the framework for recognizing and evaluating an *argument*. When you are trying to comprehend something you do not understand or to evaluate someone else's explanation, you use the framework for developing and evaluating an *explanation*.

In an explanation, you are seeking understanding. You start with a question and then explore evidence that answers the question. With an explanation you are not trying to prove a conclusion. You are simply trying to find the best explanation possible.

An explanation can communicate what something is for or how to use something, define something, make something clear, or answer what caused something. We will be focusing particularly on explanations that help you to understand the *causes* of a situation.

What Is the Communicator's Intent?

Distinguishing between arguments and explanations can be confusing also because some statements can appear to be both. The difference is in the context and the speaker's or writer's intent. If evidence is given to *support a conclusion*, it is an argument. If evidence is given to *answer a question*, it is an explanation. We must use good judgment to discern the difference.

Example:

The question is:

> *"Why did the marketing effort fail?"*

The explanation is:

> *"We both agree that the marketing effort has failed, and I think it is because the wrong customer base was targeted."*

An argument about the above topic might be:

> *"I suggest that the marketing effort has failed. We can conclude this from the lack of response from customers."*

These statements imply a lack of agreement that the marketing effort failed, and they *argue* that it has failed.

Sometimes explanations and arguments work together. An explanation can provide evidence in support of an argument. The main point is to determine the *intention* behind what is being presented. Is the intention to convince someone to adopt a point of view or is the intention to reach understanding about an agreed-upon question? This part explores the latter—developing and evaluating explanations.

EXPLANATION OR ARGUMENT?

For each of the following, put an **E** next to the statements you think might be explanations and an **A** next to the statements you think might be arguments.

1. ____ *"We both agree that work has slowed down. I think it has been happening because of the reorganization."*

   ____ *"I think we have less work in the department. It is shown by the fact that we are all taking longer breaks."*

2. ____ *"You asked why people like to visit our Web site? I guess it is because of the great graphics."*

   ____ *"We have had a huge number of hits on our Web site. This demonstrates that we have a popular site."*

3. ____ *"This project may seem complicated, but if you understand what is really wanted, it is easy. Therefore, it should not take as long as you think."*

   ____ *"I suppose the reason this project seems so complicated is because of all the different types of stakeholders involved in it."*

4. ____ *"I wonder if I should go to that meeting? No, I should skip it because making that service call is more important."*

   ____ *"I missed the meeting so that I could make a service call."*

5. ____ *"It is clear to everyone that the client is very conservative. I think the reason is that he has been burned by risky investments in the past."*

   ____ *"In my opinion, the client is very conservative—he rarely makes a risky investment."*

Compare your answers to the author's suggested responses in the Appendix.

Formulating Explanations

With a clearer understanding of the difference between arguments and explanations, you can learn how to develop explanations. As you now know, discerning the speaker's or writer's *intent* signals the difference. Explanations are not intended to convince; explanations seek to answer questions or evaluate answers to questions.

The four elements for developing an explanation are:

Element 1: *Gathering Information*

Element 2: *Processing Information*

Element 3: *Developing Hypotheses*

Element 4: *Testing Hypotheses*

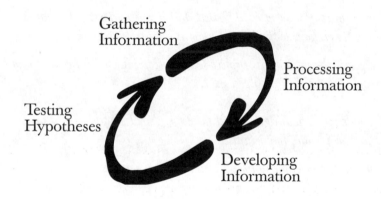

In actual practice the different elements can occur simultaneously, but we will examine them one at a time.

Element 1: Gathering Information

The first step in developing or evaluating an explanation is to gather as much information about the situation as possible.

Four points to remember when gathering information are:

1. Get as much detail as possible.

2. Pursue as many resources as possible.

3. Be alert to the type of information you look for.

   ➤ What you pay attention to will ultimately determine your explanation.

   ➤ Look for information that might not fit your initial hypothesis.

4. As you refine your hypothesis, continue to gather more information.

Sources of Information

Seek evidence for an explanation from a variety of sources, including:

➤ **Personal experience:** Your or others' observations. When evaluating evidence, be careful to assess credibility as discussed on pages 54–56. And watch out for hearsay and secondhand reports.

➤ **Documents:** Statistical information, reports, and other writings.

➤ **Artifacts:** Any relevant physical materials such as office equipment, products, software, or other manufactured goods.

Phillipe and the Delivery Slowdown

Phillipe works for a large outdoor-furniture manufacturer. He is the leader of a team responsible for fulfilling orders that come in over the Internet. For some reason, the time to delivery has increased by 20%. Phillipe is worried and would like to find an explanation for the slowdown.

If Phillipe were a non-critical thinker, he would just grab onto the easiest explanation. He might think, "Allison has been out sick for two weeks. That must be the problem. I just have to wait until she gets back."

If he were to go through the steps for gathering information, however, he would work harder to discover all the facts. Phillipe would observe each step of the process to get more personal experience and he would ask questions of co-workers to understand their experiences with order fulfillment.

He would gather any relevant documents, such as a report on the number of orders compared to previous time periods. He would study the Web site (an artifact) to determine if any glitches exist. Phillipe would avoid making any initial limiting assumptions so he could find as many avenues as possible for information.

Element 2: Processing Information

Processing information involves taking action with it. You manipulate it, grapple with it, and reflect upon it.

Follow these steps to help you process information:

➤ Take as much time as possible to reflect on the information.

➤ Compare and contrast different pieces of information.

➤ Look for patterns or unifying principles.

➤ Experiment with placing the information into different headings.

Generalizing Information

As you manipulate, grapple with, and reflect upon information you gather, it is common to form generalizations. You make a generalization when you derive a general concept from specific items. You infer that some characteristic from that specific item holds for the larger group.

Example:

Steve, a computer salesman, is interested in breaking into a new market. He has noticed that his company does not do any business with associations. Steve wonders why. He wants to know: Why doesn't the company have any association business?

So he goes to meet a prospective customer, the operations manager at a large association. As Steve walks through the building to a conference room, he notices that the office staff are using very old computers. He also notices that all the staff are dressed in conservative business attire. The operations manager greets Steve in a reserved and formal manner. The conversation is cordial, but as it continues, the prospects for a large sale do not seem promising.

Later in the week, Steve visits another director of operations at another association. He notices a very similar, conservative environment and receives a similar response. Steve continues researching his question and talks to several other salespeople who have had similar experiences.

Steve makes the generalization that large associations tend to be financially conservative and lack the commitment to large-scale computer investments. This generalization forms the foundation of a concept or mental model Steve now has about associations.

Such a generalization about associations might be helpful to Steve as he tries to break into another market. But it could also lead him astray because he has made the generalization from limited experience and research. Forming a mental model from too small a sample is called *overgeneralization*, a common error in information processing.

Information Processing Errors

As you observed in the above example, looking for patterns and groupings in the information you gather is an important part of processing information. But it can lead to errors in reasoning, including these common pitfalls:

> **Stereotyping**

> **Self-delusion**

> **Attribution error**

> **Excessive focus on the conspicuous**

As you learn about each pitfall and read the examples, consider a time you might have made a similar error in processing information at work.

Stereotyping

When your initial mental model is incorrect, biased, or incomplete, you may develop a stereotype. Whatever impression you have of the initial group gets assigned to the entire group and becomes the explanation.

Example:

People who work with numbers have poor interpersonal skills.

Self-Delusion

When your personal biases flavor your perceptions, you may become deluded in your thinking.

Example:

Steve, the computer salesman, has not made a sale in weeks. He visits a long-term customer who implies that he is not interested in purchasing at this time. Steve's desperation deludes him into misinterpreting the customer's signals as an invitation to pursue the sale, and he becomes overly pushy, potentially harming his relationship with the client.

Attribution Error

When you explain other people's behavior as being based on internal variables—personality qualities, habits—rather than outside situational variables, you are making an error in attribution.

Example:

When a phone call is not returned promptly, you think it is because the other person is rude, rather than thinking perhaps the person never received the message or is simply overloaded with work.

Or if co-workers oppose one of your ideas in a meeting, you may attribute the opposition to their internal characteristics, such as stubbornness or irrationality, rather than the possibility that the idea would not work.

Excessive Focus on the Conspicuous

When you focus more than is appropriate on particularly vivid or memorable data.

Example:

A workgroup of 18 employees has two aggressive complainers. When the workgroup's main project is late, after the original project plan was altered, you explain it by saying that you have a lot of resistant employees with bad attitudes.

Element 3: Developing Hypotheses

The purpose of an explanation is to provide a well-reasoned answer to a question about why something is so—what caused it. As we gather and process information, we begin to develop answers to the question at hand by making a speculation—a hypothesis—to guide our questioning. When we think we have a possible answer, we research it further.

A hypothesis is a tentative statement that proposes a possible explanation to some phenomenon or event. It is a *provisional* explanation for why something occurred.

To develop a hypothesis, you look at different possible categories and the qualities associated with them and see which ones best fit the facts you have about the topic. Then you seek more facts as you pursue the best possible hypothesis. Your goal is to develop a hypothesis that accounts for as much of the relevant facts as possible.

Generating Alternatives

When we develop hypotheses, it is easy to accept the first one we think of. But the first idea is not necessarily the best one. Often several interpretations are possible. Expanding our investigation to look at alternatives gives us a richer field from which to draw a good hypothesis.

We also can get caught up in thinking there are only two alternatives—a solution is either black or white. But most situations are not so limited. Often many alternatives exist.

Phillipe's Delivery Slowdown Hypotheses

In an earlier example (page 76), Phillipe at the outdoor-furniture company comprehensively gathered information about why his team was slower at fulfilling Internet orders.

His initial explanation was that the slowdown was from the two-week absence of one of his workers. Being a critical thinker, however, Phillipe began to process the information by comparing and contrasting pieces of information to find patterns. As he did this he formed several hypotheses for why order fulfillment was 20% slower:

➤ Even though there was a temporary replacement, Allison's two-week absence and the replacement's lack of experience created a hole in the process that slowed everything down.

➤ The new Web site request form was poorly written, so it solicited confusing requests from customers, which slowed down the order-fulfillment rate.

➤ Because it was summertime, people performed more slowly than at other times of the year.

➤ Inventory was low, creating a backup of orders.

Phillipe developed these alternative hypotheses as he gathered and processed relevant information.

HYPOTHESIZING AT WORK

Think of the most difficult challenge coming up for you at work. Develop a hypothesis of why this is going to occur. Do not go with the easiest explanation. Generate at least four possible alternatives.

Upcoming Challenge

_____

_____

_____

_____

Alternative Hypotheses

1. _____

_____

_____

2. _____

_____

_____

3. _____

_____

_____

4. _____

_____

_____

Element 4: Testing Hypotheses

Once you develop a hypothesis, you can test it to see if it is consistent with all the evidence. At the same time, look for evidence that might invalidate the hypothesis.

Comparing and Evaluating Hypotheses

In addition to testing your hypothesis, you also should seek to discover if some alternative hypothesis fits the evidence better. Find out which one has the least number of assumptions associated with it.

As you process the information and grapple with possible explanations, you refine and modify the initial hypothesis. Thus, the shape of the hypothesis is adjusted as more facts and understandings come to light.

Ultimately, a good hypothesis will:

➤ Appear believable

➤ Explain all the relevant facts

➤ Be better than alternative explanations in giving clear reasons for the situation (because the alternatives do not cover the facts as well)

The Testing of a Hypothesis

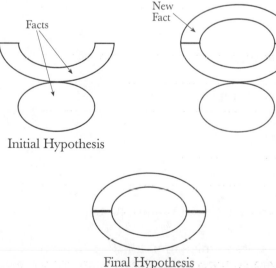

Facts

Initial Hypothesis

New Fact

Final Hypothesis
(Explanation)

Asking Discovery Questions

Giving thought to explanations is a process of discovery. The best way to develop explanations is to ask questions. Assertive questions push us beyond the initial statement to better understand the strength of an explanation.

Here are some assertive questions you can ask at each stage in the development of an explanation.

1. Gathering Information

➤ What do I know about this situation?

➤ What kind of information do I need?

➤ What information is most important?

2. Processing Information

➤ Have I dealt with this kind of situation before? How did I solve it before?

➤ How can I categorize this information?

➤ What are the patterns?

3. Developing Hypotheses

➤ What is my hypothesis?

➤ What are the alternatives in this situation?

➤ What alternative makes the most sense?

4. Testing Hypotheses

➤ Is the hypothesis believable?

➤ Does any information not fit into the hypothesis?

➤ Is this the simplest explanation for the situation?

➤ Is this hypothesis better than any other possible hypothesis?

DEVELOPING AN EXPLANATION AT WORK

Pick an aspect of your work that you want to be able to explain. Go through these discovery questions from the previous page to help you form your explanation.

1. Gathering Information

What do I know about this situation?

_____

_____

What kind of information do I need?

_____

_____

What information is most important?

_____

_____

2. Processing Information

Have I dealt with this kind of situation before? How did I solve it before?

_____

_____

How can I categorize this information?

_____

_____

What are the patterns?

_____

_____

CONTINUED

3. Developing Hypotheses

What is my hypothesis?

_____

_____

What are the alternatives in this situation?

_____

_____

What alternative makes the most sense?

_____

_____

4. Testing Hypotheses

Is the hypothesis believable?

_____

_____

Does any information not fit into the hypothesis?

_____

_____

Is this the simplest explanation for the situation?

_____

_____

Is this hypothesis better than any other possible hypothesis?

_____

_____

Challenging Assumptions

To develop the strongest and most accurate explanations possible, we must become aware of biases and unspoken assumptions that might cloud our reasoning. Such beliefs grow out of the explanations we develop about how the world works.

Assumptions are beliefs that are presumed. They are usually unstated beliefs that support expressed reasoning.

We are constantly using assumptions. They help us make decisions.

"I assume I have a job when I go in to work."

But there is a balance. Assumptions are often taken for granted even though they can greatly influence the conclusion. So it helps to be aware of the assumptions operating and to evaluate them to ferret out biases or erroneous beliefs.

Phillipe's Assumptions

As Phillipe tries to explain his order fulfillment slowdown at the outdoor-furniture company (pages 76 and 81), he seems to be making the following initial assumptions:

➤ A 20% slowdown is unusual for his business process.

➤ A 20% slowdown is a problem that needs to be addressed.

➤ Phillipe has the ability to figure out an explanation for the slowdown.

These are reasonable assumptions for Phillipe, which shows that making assumptions helps to direct attempts to reach explanations.

But if Phillipe were new to his job and unaware that a 20% slowdown is a common fluctuation for order fulfillment, then he would be operating under an erroneous assumption. He could discover this error as he gathered and processed information on his way to formulating an explanation.

CASE STUDY: Identify the Assumptions

See if you can recognize the assumptions Phillipe made in each of his possible hypotheses as follows:

1. Even though there was a temporary replacement, Allison's two-week absence and the replacement's lack of experience created a hole in the process that slowed everything down.

   Underlying assumptions:

   _____

   _____

2. The new Web site request form was poorly written and it solicited confusing requests from customers, which slowed down the order-fulfillment rate.

   Underlying assumptions:

   _____

   _____

3. Because it was summertime, people performed more slowly than at other times of the year.

   Underlying assumptions:

   _____

   _____

4. Inventory was low, creating a backup of orders.

   Underlying assumptions:

   _____

   _____

Compare your answers to the author's suggested responses in the Appendix.

A P P E N D I X

Reviewing What You've Learned

Critical thinking is a way of life. In Part 1 you explored the attitudes and strategies for becoming a critical thinker. Parts 2 and 3 gave you two frameworks to apply to statements and decisions you face. These frameworks are:

The Steps for Recognizing and Evaluating Arguments

Step 1: *Pinpointing Issues*

Step 2: *Identifying Arguments*

Step 3: *Seeking Clarity*

Step 4: *Understanding Context*

Step 5: *Finding Credibility*

Step 6: *Looking for Consistency*

Step 7: *Judging Arguments*

The Elements for Developing and Evaluating Explanations

Element 1: *Gathering Information*

Element 2: *Processing Information*

Element 3: *Developing Hypotheses*

Element 4: *Testing Hypotheses*

Take the time to think about your intentions and the intentions of those around you when you are grappling with a problem.

Are you trying to convince someone about your point of view? Are co-workers trying to convince you about their opinions? If so, apply the steps for developing and evaluating arguments.

Do you want to understand and explain a situation? If so, apply the steps for developing and evaluating explanations.

As you become more and more familiar with these two frameworks, the skills will become more refined and automatic, and you will find yourself living fully as a critical thinker.

PERSONAL ACTION PLAN

Which critical thinking style do I most want to develop in myself? (See page 20.)

_____

Which strategies will I practice to improve my critical thinking skills? (See page 24.)

_____

_____

I will practice the seven steps for recognizing and evaluating arguments (page 37) in the following ways:

_____

_____

_____

_____

_____

_____

I will practice the four steps to developing and evaluating explanations (page 74) in the following ways:

_____

_____

_____

_____

_____

_____

Author's Suggested Responses to Exercises

Non-Critical Styles in Action (page 18)

1. Zack is demonstrating the non-critical thinking style of "the Snob" by arrogantly discounting Juanita's skills.

2. Holly shows signs of using the non-critical thinking style of "the Leech." She accepted uncritically whatever was being said to her without making the effort to form her own views.

3. The senior executive is using the non-critical thinking style of "the Dilettante." He is being overly receptive and giving vague reasons for an inadequately evaluated line of action that may well cause great difficulties in the future.

Critical Thinking Style File (page 21)

1. Alexa is demonstrating the critical thinking styles of the Navigator and the Warrior. She is looking ahead to choose the best path and is courageous in speaking up and not going along with the team leader.

2. Pascal is showing the critical thinking styles of the Student and the Detective. He wants to get more information and to inquire further about the basis for the recommendations before jumping into them.

3. Steven is using the critical thinking styles of the Explorer and the Detective. He is going to proactively seek the truth and ask relevant questions.

4. Hans is showing the critical thinking styles of the Explorer and the Warrior. He is curious in looking for the truth and is willing to jump in and tackle a potentially difficult situation.

Rephrasing for Clarity (page 49)

1. Many employees expressed insecurity about their jobs after the cutbacks, and this negatively effected performance.

2. You mentioned my name only in passing, which implied I was only peripherally involved on the project. Please correct this by acknowledging my integral involvement.

3. Employees spending an excessive amount of time on the phone on personal business have hindered the department's overall productivity.

Explanation or Argument? (page 73)

1. **E** *"We both agree that work has slowed down. I think it has been happening because of the reorganization."*

    This is probably an explanation. The parties appear to agree about the topic in question. The question is "Why has work slowed down?" and the answer is "Because of the reorganization."

    A *"I think we have less work in the department. It is shown by the fact that we are all taking longer breaks."*

    This appears to be an argument because the speaker seems to be trying to prove that the conclusion, "We have less work in the department," is being supported by the evidence, "We are all taking longer breaks."

2. **E** *"You asked why people like to visit our Web site? I guess it is because of the great graphics."*

    This is an explanation because there is an attempt to understand the question "Why do people like to visit our Web site?" The answer is "Because of the great graphics."

    A *"We have had a huge number of hits on our Web site. This demonstrates that we have a popular Web site."*

    Here the speaker is trying to prove that his conclusion, "We have a popular Web site," is supported by the evidence of the huge number of hits.

3. **A** *"This project may seem complicated, but if you understand what is really wanted, it is easy. Therefore, it should not take as long as you think."*

    This is an argument because the speaker is trying to convince the listener that the project is easier and should not take as long as thought.

    E *"I suppose the reason this project seems so complicated is because of all the different types of stakeholders involved."*

    This appears to be an explanation: The question "Why does this project seem so complicated?" is answered by "There are many different types of stakeholders involved."

4. **A** *"I wonder if I should go to that meeting? No, I should skip it because making that service call is more important."*

This person is arguing with herself over attending the meeting. She makes the argument that she should skip the meeting.

   E *"I missed the meeting so that I could make a service call."*

This appears to be an explanation in which the unspoken question is "Why did you miss the meeting?" The answer is "To make a service call."

5. **E** *"It is clear to everyone that the client is very conservative. I think the reason is that he has been burned by risky investments in the past."*

Everyone agrees the client is very conservative. The unspoken question in this explanation is "Why?" The explanation given is "He has been burned by risky investments in the past."

   A *"In my opinion, the client is very conservative because he rarely makes a risky investment."*

This seems to be an argument rather than an explanation. The opinion, "The client is very conservative," is supported by the evidence, "He rarely makes a risky investment."

Author's Suggested Responses to the Case Studies

What Is the Issue? (page 41)

Issue:

The issue from Jeff's point of view is: Should I continue to work with George?

From Doris' perspective, the issue is: What can be done to solve the problem?

Conclusion:

Neither Jeff nor Doris sought to clarify the issue under discussion. This misunderstanding may lead to unnecessary tension.

New Faces (page 44)

The issue could be stated: "Has a change in the level of friendliness among employees affected the company's productivity?"

The conclusion presented by the letter writer could be stated: "A decrease in friendliness between staff is hurting the company's efficiency."

Moving Toward the Internet (page 46)

Issue:

The issue can be stated as "Should the company shift its strategic direction and capital investment to place a greater focus on Internet sales?"

Conclusion:

The conclusion could be stated as "Acme, Inc., should shift its strategic direction and capital investment to focus more heavily on Internet sales."

Evidence:

➤ A greater number of people are getting on the Internet and becoming more comfortable using it to do business.

➤ Acme's Internet sales have dramatically increased.

➤ Acme's traditional sales have decreased.

➤ The traditional methods are more expensive to operate than the Internet services.

Review

Once you have pinpointed the issue and identified the argument, then you can decide if the issue is important enough for you to spend the time to analyze the argument.

If the issue is one you want to explore further, then you must evaluate the evidence and analyze how the components of the argument fit together.

What's Behind the Statement? (page 51)

There are several possible motives and purposes.

1. Bartlett is a nice guy and likes to help people.

2. Bartlett hates doing the status reports and has been pressured by his supervisor for months to get the status reports done and would love to hand them over to you.

3. Bartlett's enthusiasm is misplaced, and he is unknowingly giving you erroneous information.

To assess the speaker's motive and purpose:

➤ Do not respond immediately.

➤ Research the statements of the person.

➤ Ask questions about the speaker's relationships within the office.

Responding to the case study:

➤ Before taking on the status reports, talk to your manager and ask if this is really part of your responsibility.

➤ Ask Bartlett for more specific details.

➤ Ask other colleagues about Bartlett.

Should You Accept the Proposal? (page 61)

Issue:

Should the submissions division move toward solely using electronic submissions?

Conclusion:

Yes, the submissions division should move toward solely using electronic submissions.

Evidence:

1. Data storage is becoming cumbersome and expensive.

2. The current method of cataloging, handling, and so on is inefficient and prone to error.

3. No data would be lost using only electronic submissions.

4. The Internet technology that would facilitate electronic submissions is readily available to the entire customer base.

5. The electronic submissions would be properly organized so they could be placed directly into the database without requiring staff for data entry.

6. Customers would get immediate acknowledgment of the receipt of their submissions.

7. The system would quickly identify delinquent or errant submissions.

8. The initiative will provide the opportunity to modernize out-of-date databases.

9. The burden on the staff would be reduced so they could focus on other responsibilities.

Analysis:

1. Is the evidence clear and unambiguous?

   Evidence #4 states that the necessary Internet technology is "readily available" to the entire customer base. What exactly is meant by "readily available"? Is it available but costly? Is it available only to high-tech companies?

   Evidence #8 mentions the initiative providing the opportunity to "modernize" out-of-date databases. What does "modernize" mean for specific time and resource commitment? How much of an extra expense will this create?

2. Does the context strengthen or weaken the evidence?

You have to wonder if the head of the information technology department, who is championing this initiative, has some hidden motives that bias the decision to push for it.

3. Is the evidence credible?

As a member of the submissions department, you may have specific knowledge that would make you suspicious of some of the evidence about the current methods' inefficiency and the ease of transitioning to a new methodology. Knowing the complexity of the task, you may question the implication that there would be less of a burden on the staff. And the task force may have been lacking in the expertise needed to understand the submissions division. Was the task force accurately informed?

4. Are all the pieces of evidence consistent with each other?

The different pieces of evidence are fairly consistent with each other.

5. Does the evidence support the conclusions?

If all of the pieces of evidence were strong, they would support the conclusions. After the analysis, however, a number of serious questions need to be answered before you should accept the argument.

Identify the Assumptions (page 88)

1. Even though there was a temporary replacement, Allison's two-week absence and the replacement's lack of experience created a hole in the process that slowed everything down.

   Underlying assumptions:

   ➤ The replacement works at a slower pace than Allison does.

   ➤ Experience is needed for the replacement to work as fast as Allison.

2. The new Web site request form was poorly written and it solicited confusing requests from customers, which slowed down the order-fulfillment rate.

   Underlying assumptions:

   ➤ Confusing requests would slow down the order-fulfillment rate.

3. Because it was summertime, people performed more slowly than at other times of the year.

   Underlying assumptions:

   ➤ Fluctuating performance is bad.

   ➤ Performance fluctuates with different seasons.

4. Inventory was low and this created a backup of orders.

   Underlying assumptions:

   ➤ A backup of orders automatically means the order-fulfillment rate would be slower.

These underlying assumptions may be true or not. Being aware of them, though, can lead you to seek out new data to assess the truth of each assumption. By challenging your underlying assumptions, you refine and improve your ability to evaluate an explanation.

Additional Reading

Bono, Edward de. *de Bono's Thinking Course*. New York: Facts on File, Inc., 1994.

Capaldi, Nicholas. *The Art of Deception*. Amherst, NY: Prometheus Books, 1987.

Chaffee, John. *The Thinker's Way*. Boston: Little, Brown & Co., 1998.

Diestler, Sherry. *Becoming A Critical Thinker: A User Friendly Manual*. Upper Saddle River, NJ: Prentice Hall, 1998.

Ennis, Robert H. *Critical Thinking*. Upper Saddle River, NJ: Prentice Hall, 1996.

Gellatt, H.B. *Creative Decision Making*. Crisp Series, 2002.

Gilovich, Thomas. *How We Know What Isn't So: The Fallibility of Human Reason in Everyday Life*. New York: The Free Press, 1991.

Hoaglund, John. *Critical Thinking*. Newport News, VA: Vale Press, 1999.

Kindler, Herb. *Clear and Creative Thinking*. Crisp Series, 2002.

Nothstine, William L. *Influencing Others*. Crisp Series, 1989.

Zuker, Elaina. *Influence*. Crisp Series, 1994.

Also Available

Books•Videos•Computer-Based Training Products

If you enjoyed this book, we have great news for you. There are over 200 books available in the *Crisp Fifty-Minute™ Series*. For more information visit us online at www.axzopress.com

Subject Areas Include:

Management
Human Resources
Communication Skills
Personal Development
Sales/Marketing
Finance
Coaching and Mentoring
Customer Service/Quality
Small Business and Entrepreneurship
Training
Life Planning
Writing

VERQ